Wealth Of Nations

India

Jen Green

HODDER
Wayland

an imprint of Hodder Children's Books

Wealth Of Nations series includes:

Bangladesh   India

Brazil   Nigeria

Cover: Main photo: the Taj Mahal. Inset: colourful saris in Rajistan.

Title page: Bicycles and cycle rickshaws in the city of Jaipur.

Contents page: The desert in Rajistan.

India is a simplified version of the title *India* in Wayland's *Economically Developing Countries* series.

Text copyright © 2000 Hodder Wayland
Volume copyright © 2000 Hodder Wayland

Series editor: Polly Goodman

First published in Great Britain in 1995 by Wayland Publishers Ltd. This edition published in 2000 by Hodder Wayland, an imprint of Hodder Children's Books.

A Catalogue record for this book is available from the British Library.

ISBN 0 7502 3066 5

Printed and bound by G. Canale & C. S.p.A. Turin, Italy

Hodder Children's Books
A division of Hodder Headline plc
338 Euston Road, London NW1 3BH

Picture acknowledgements
The publisher would like to thank the following for allowing their photographs to be reproduced in this book: Actionaid (Liba Taylor) 39, 40, 41; Actionaid 42, 43; Camera Press 9 (Dinodia), 15 (top and bottom), 35; David Cumming 1, 3, 4 (top), 6, 10, 11, 14, 17, 18, 19, 20, 21, 23, 24, 25, 26, 27, 28, 31, 32, 34, 36, 38, 44, 45; Eye Ubiquitous 8 (Martin Reeves), 16 (David Cumming), 33 (Jason Burke), 37 (C Johnson); (Chris Gibb) 7; Peter Newark's Historical Pictures 13; Zul, Chapel Studios 22, 29.
Photographs on pages 4 (bottom), 12 and 30 come from the Wayland Picture Library. All artwork by Peter Bull.

CONTENTS

INTRODUCTION

India is a large country in southern Asia. Pakistan and Bangladesh used to be part of India, but in 1947, the country was divided.

India has a population of almost a billion people. After China, it is the most densely populated country in the world. About one in every six people in the world comes from India.

India is a mixture of old and new. It has modern industries and technology. But many Indians are very poor and still farm the land using traditional methods.

▲ India has about 40 large cities, but most people live in the countryside.

◄ Camels are used for transport in Rajistan.

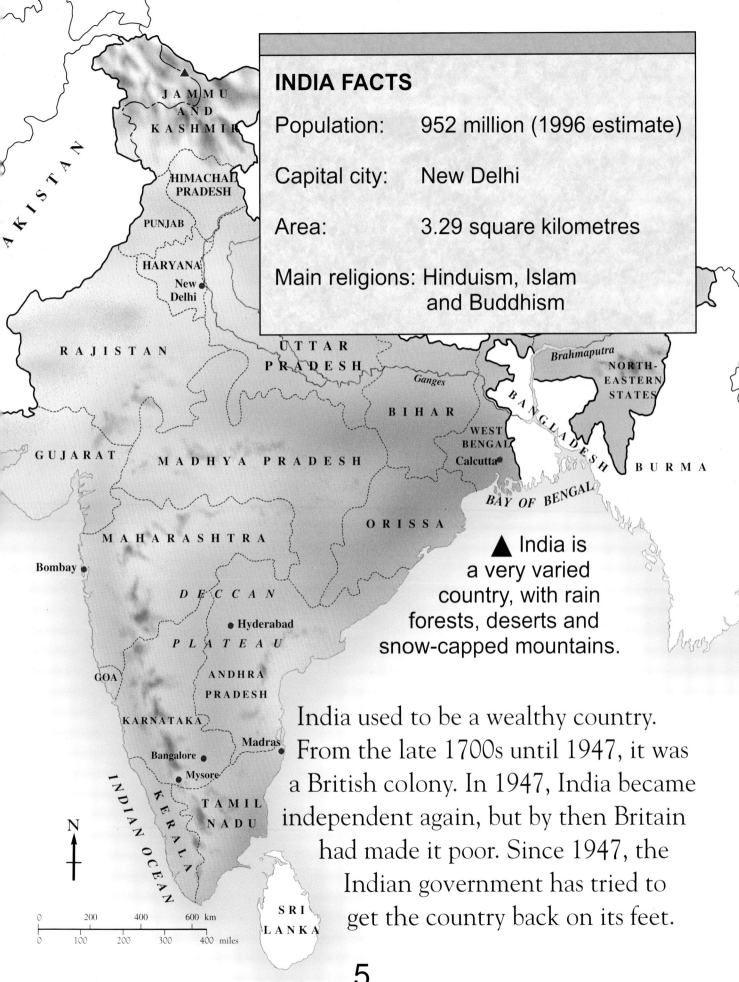

INDIA FACTS

Population: 952 million (1996 estimate)

Capital city: New Delhi

Area: 3.29 square kilometres

Main religions: Hinduism, Islam
                and Buddhism

PAKISTAN

JAMMU AND KASHMIR

HIMACHAL PRADESH

PUNJAB

HARYANA

New Delhi

RAJISTAN

UTTAR PRADESH

Ganges

Brahmaputra

NORTH-EASTERN STATES

BIHAR

WEST BENGAL

Calcutta

BANGLADESH

BURMA

GUJARAT

MADHYA PRADESH

ORISSA

BAY OF BENGAL

MAHARASHTRA

Bombay

DECCAN

Hyderabad

PLATEAU

GOA

ANDHRA PRADESH

KARNATAKA

Madras

Bangalore

Mysore

KERALA

TAMIL NADU

INDIAN OCEAN

N

SRI LANKA

0   200   400   600 km
0 100   200   300   400 miles

▲ India is
a very varied
country, with rain
forests, deserts and
snow-capped mountains.

India used to be a wealthy country.
From the late 1700s until 1947, it was
a British colony. In 1947, India became
independent again, but by then Britain
had made it poor. Since 1947, the
Indian government has tried to
get the country back on its feet.

5

LAND AND CLIMATE

India is the seventh-largest country in the world. It covers 3,287,263 square kilometres.

India can be divided into three main regions. In the far north lie the Himalayas, the world's highest mountains. South of the Himalayas, the northern plains are watered by mighty rivers such as the Ganges and the Indus. Most of southern India is taken up by a high plateau called the Deccan Plateau.

The best farmland in India is on the northern plains. The land there is irrigated by water raised from the rivers.

◀ In Ladakh, northern India, water from the Indus river is used to irrigate farmland.

CLIMATE

India has three seasons. Winter lasts from October to February. In many areas the weather is warm and dry. Spring lasts from March to May. In spring the weather is hot and dry.

▲ Monsoon rains sometimes bring floods to many parts of India.

RAINFALL AND THE MONSOON

Summer (June to September) is the main rainy season. The temperature is very hot. A moist, seasonal wind called the monsoon blows in from the Indian Ocean, bringing rain. It soaks the south first, around the end of May, and then moves north to reach the north-west by July.

AVERAGE SEASONAL RAINFALL

	New Dehli	Madras
Winter (Oct to Feb)	64 mm	847 mm
Spring (Mar to May)	34 mm	48 mm
Summer (June to Sept)	544 mm	375 mm
TOTAL	642 mm	1,270 mm

Farmers depend on the monsoon rains. The monsoon brings 70 per cent of all the rain that falls on India each year. Many areas are dry for eight months of the year.

Only 20 per cent of India's farmland can be irrigated by water drawn up from rivers. The rest of the land relies on the monsoon rains.

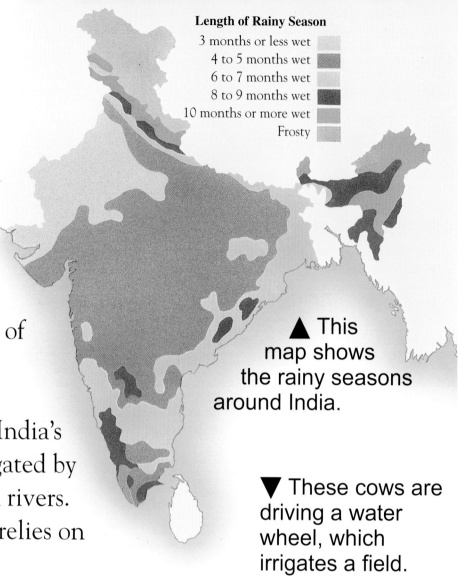

Length of Rainy Season
3 months or less wet
4 to 5 months wet
6 to 7 months wet
8 to 9 months wet
10 months or more wet
Frosty

▲ This map shows the rainy seasons around India.

▼ These cows are driving a water wheel, which irrigates a field.

MONSOON RAINS
Sometimes the monsoon rains do harm as well as good. Some years, the monsoon arrives early and causes floods. The floods wash land away, and people and animals can drown.

In other years, the monsoon arrives late and brings hardly any rain. Cattle die of thirst, fields dry up and food is scarce.

◄ Earthquakes are another hazard in India. This man is clearing up after an earthquake in 1993.

EARTHQUAKES

Earthquakes are quite common in India. They are very destructive. In 1993, a major earthquake hit south-west India. It killed 7,600 people and destroyed 18,800 homes.

EFFECTS OF BRITISH RULE

Some people think that India was a backward country before Europeans arrived. In fact, India has a long, proud history that stretches back for centuries.

▲ This is an observatory in New Dehli, which was built in 1725. It was used to check the work of ancient Indian astronomers.

ANCIENT CIVILIZATIONS

In ancient times, India was home to some of the world's earliest civilisations. Hundreds of years ago, Indian astronomers knew that the world was round, and divided the year into 365.4 days. Indian mathematicians invented the decimal system and performed complicated equations.

When Europeans first visited India, they came partly to learn, for India led the way in many sciences.

Around 325 BC, Indian factories were the first to make iron and high-quality steel, called *wootz*. The process of making steel was complicated and needed very high temperatures. A famous *wootz* pillar in the Quitab Minar, a building in Delhi, does not have a speck of rust on it, though it is 1,600 years old.

Indian society was very well organized before the Europeans arrived. Farmers grew enough crops to feed everyone. Doctors healed the sick with medicines made from herbs.

Schools lay within reach of every village, and many people could read. Three major religions, Hinduism, Islam and Buddhism, flourished. India also had many skilled artists and craftspeople.

◀ This iron pillar in Delhi is still rust-free, although it has been in the open air for over 1,600 years.

THE BRITISH ARRIVE

Europeans arrived in India from the 1500s. They came mainly to trade. In 1600, the British government gave a British trading company called the East India Company permission to be the only British firm to trade with India.

The map shows:
- British Territory by 1805.
- Indian states mainly allied with Britain.
- British Territory after 1856.

KASHMIR

PUNJAB

RAJPUT LANDS

BENGAL

Calcutta

Bombay

Madras

▲ This map shows areas under British control from 1805 until 1947.

The owners of the East India Company aimed to make as much money as possible from India. They opened offices and factories in India, and used their own army to protect them. Soon the soldiers were being used to conquer Indian rulers who did not want to trade with the company.

◄ This drawing shows Indians being hanged and shot at by cannons.

By 1800, the East India Company controlled much of India. Indians who defied British rule were often killed in brutal ways.

FARMS DESTROYED

The East India Company made farmers pay a high land tax which took half of their earnings. Farmers who could not pay were forced to sell their land to rich landowners, and then pay rent to farm. Those who could not pay rent were turned off the land. Many farms became unoccupied and went to waste.

To make more profit, the East India Company forced farmers to grow crops for sale abroad, such as cotton and tea. Less crops were grown for food, so no extra food was stored in case of drought. When the rains failed, many people starved.

The company also cut down many of India's rain forests to build ships and railway lines.

Many people starved to ▶ death during droughts in the 1770s.

Art and sculpture ▶ flourished in India before the British came, as this temple carving shows.

SCHOOLS

The East India Company's land tax also affected schools. Most schools had their own land, but they could not afford the new tax, so many had to shut.

PROFIT FOR BRITAIN

For almost 200 years, the company plundered India's resources and gave very little back. It built a good railway network, but only to help send Indian goods to Britain.

In the 1780s, some British members of parliament forced the British government to shut down the East India Company and take over the running of India. But by then, it was too late. Once India had been a thriving country. Now many farms were ruined and most people were poor.

INDEPENDENCE

By 1900, many Indian people wanted their country to become independent from Britain. During the 1920s, an Indian lawyer, called Mahatma Gandhi, demanded independence on behalf of the Indian people.

▲ Police break up a protest against British rule in the 1930s.

The British finally left in 1947, but now, over fifty years later, India has still not recovered from their unjust rule. India is independent, but it will take many years for the scars of British rule to heal.

MAHATMA GANDHI

Gandhi studied law in Britain and worked in South Africa, before returning to India. He led the Indian people in peaceful protests against British rule, which eventually forced the British to leave. He was known as Mahatma, which means 'great soul'.

◄ Gandhi lived and dressed very simply.

15

MEASURING POVERTY

People often talk about 'rich' and 'poor' countries. Poor countries are often called 'developing' countries. Rich nations are 'developed' countries. One way of finding out if a country is rich or poor is to measure the total wealth the country produces and then divide that figure by the population. This is is called the Gross National Product (GNP) per person. The chart below shows the GNP of various countries.

▼ In India a few people are rich, but most, such as this rickshaw puller, are poor.

GROSS NATIONAL PRODUCT (GNP) PER PERSON

World rank		GNP
1	Switzerland	36,080
6	USA	23,240
16	UK	17,790
115	India	310
123	Bangladesh	220
132	Mozambique	60

▲ Many people are desperately poor in India. In big cities like Calcutta, people beg for food.

The chart on page 16 shows Switzerland has the highest GNP per person in the world. India comes 115th out of 132 countries. It is one of the world's poorest nations. The GNP shows the money each person would get if all the wealth was shared equally. In fact, some people are richer, while others are poor.

BASIC PROBLEMS
According to some experts, for a country to be called developed, there should be no poverty, unemployment or inequality.

In practise, no country can completely wipe out these problems, but in developed countries they exist on a much smaller scale. Like other developing countries, India has more than its fair share of these three important problems.

◄ Many schools in India do not have enough desks or textbooks.

POVERTY IN INDIA

One way of measuring poverty is to find out the number of people who lack the basic necessities of life, such as clean water, enough food, health care and education.

▼ In India, many people struggle to earn enough to buy food.

According to this measure, India has hundreds of millions of poor people. Experts think 48 per cent of India's people are poor, compared to 18 per cent in Britain.

NOT ENOUGH FOOD

Experts believe that 63 per cent of children in India do not get enough of the right type of food. They are called malnourished. Bangladesh, on India's eastern border, is the only country in the world where the problem is worse.

18

POVERTY IN INDIA

- On average, Indian women live to the age of 62 years, and Indian men to 61. In the USA, women live to 80, and men to 73.

- In India, 52 per cent of adults cannot read or write. This compares to less than 5 per cent in European countries.

- Only 73 per cent of India's people have access to safe drinking water. In most Western countries, everyone has access to clean water.

- In India, there are 1,000 people for each hospital bed. In Britain, there are 200.

It is hard for poor people in India to break out of their poverty. The areas where they live have few schools, so they cannot get a good education, which means they cannot get a good job when they leave school.

Poverty is one of the most difficult problems the Indian government has to tackle.

▼ These men wash on the street because their homes have no piped water.

WORK IN INDIA

India does not have enough jobs for all its people. A great many people either have no job at all, or no regular full-time work. Instead, they do odd jobs for an hour or two a week, or for one or two days each week or month.

WORK IN INDIA	Percentage of population
Farming and fishing	67%
Industry	13%
Services	20%

The Indian government believes that about 12.5 per cent of its workers are unemployed. Probably about the same number of people only work part-time. This means that about a quarter of India's workers do not receive a proper wage to feed and support their families.

In India, a large percentage of people still work on the land because there are not enough jobs in factories.

▼ These people work part-time in the market.

FEW FACTORIES

India has few factories because its industries only started to develop since Independence. The British used India as a source of cheap farm produce. The only factories they built were to prepare crops such as cotton for export to Britain.

In 1947, only 10 per cent of India's workers worked in factories. Today, the figure has only risen a little.

▼ This map shows the location of India's main industries.

Type of industry

- ○ Steel plant
- ▼ Oil and gas
- ▲ Oil refineries
- ■ Major port
- ◆ Major iron ore mine
- ✳ Petrochemical plant
- ▽ Space centre
- ◇ Shipyard
- ☐ Nuclear power station
- △ Aircraft manufacture
- ⁺⁺⁺⁺ Railway

TOO MANY WORKERS

Another reason there are few jobs in India is that the population keeps growing. During the 1980s and 1990s, the population grew by more than 2 per cent each year, which is over 19 million people. Many Indian people think that having a lot of children will make them richer. Instead, children have to be clothed, fed and educated, so families with many children are often very poor.

▲ India has many small workshops, like this one in Calcutta.

21

FARMING

Around 62 per cent of India's workers are employed in farming. A few farmers make a good living from the land, particularly on the banks of the rivers on the northern plains.

▼ A farmer's wife spreads coriander seeds on a roof to dry.

However, most farmers and farm workers are very poor. They struggle to grow enough crops to feed themselves, and have little or nothing left over to sell for profit.

In many areas, the soil is poor and the land is only watered by the monsoon. Poor farmers have no money to spend on fertilizers to improve the soil.

MODERN FARMING

Farming methods have changed a lot in the last 20 years. New types of wheat and rice have been developed, which produce bigger harvests. But they need a lot of water, fertilizers, and pesticides to kill insects.

In India, most farmers cannot afford to buy these chemicals, so the new farming methods have not helped them.

◀ Farmers in Ladakh in northern India separating the chaff (husks) from their grain by hand.

FARM WORKERS

Farm labourers earn money by working for farmers. They help to gather the harvest or sow seeds. This kind of work is available only at certain times of year, and depends on the weather. If the monsoon fails or washes away the crops, there is no work.

In India, most people live in the countryside, so the population has grown fastest there. Each year there are more workers, but only the same number of jobs, so the number of people out of work rises.

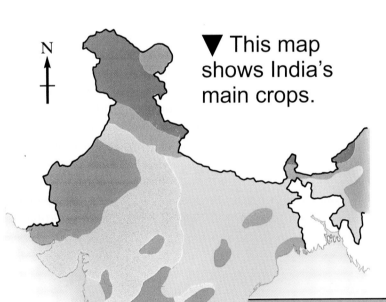

N

▼ This map shows India's main crops.

Rice

Forest

Highland pasture

Unproductive land

Wheat and maize

MONEY FROM FARMING

Each year the amount of money India earns from farming gets smaller. This sum has to be shared by more and more people, so farmers become poorer.

23

▼ Thirteen-year-old Arun sells snacks in the centre of Calcutta.

▲ This Delhi teenager works to earn extra money for his family.

CHILD WORKERS

In India, many children start work when they are still small. Since Independence, the number of child workers has increased.

In families where parents have no regular jobs, children are often sent out to work instead. There are few jobs in the villages, so children are sent to the nearest town or city. There they do any work they can find, from shoe cleaning or running errands for hotels to factory work.

'I never went to school so I cannot read or write.' – **Arun, aged 13.**

24

SOLD TO FACTORIES

When families are desperate for money, they sometimes 'sell' their children to factory owners. The employers look on the children as their slaves. They treat them badly and pay them very low wages.

Silk-weaving is an example of an industry that employs many child workers.

▶ Boys working in a silk-weaving workshop.

STREET CHILDREN OF BANGALORE

Bangalore, in southern India, is one of the country's biggest cities. It has many modern industries. Computers, electrical goods and space satellites are made there.

These new industries have made Bangalore a rich city. Despite this, over 40 per cent of the city's population lives in overcrowded slums.

Many families are so poor they are forced to send their children out to work.

Most working children end up on the streets.

There are about 45,000 street children in Bangalore. Some only work on the streets by day and go home in the evening. But over half spend their whole lives on the streets and never go home.

Some of these children are orphans who have no family to support them. Others have left home because they were unhappy there.

◄ A street child in Bangalore.

▲ These homeless people are sorting lottery tickets for a recycler, who will sell them on to a paper mill.

Some street children are teenagers. Others are only five or six years old.

Over half of all street children are 'rag pickers'. They rummage through rubbish for waste such as paper, plastic or cardboard. They pass the waste to recyclers, who sell it on to factories. The recyclers pay them a little money, or give them food and shelter.

Living on the streets is very dangerous. Some children come into contact with thieves who encourage them to start stealing. Others are kidnapped by 'slum agents', who force them to work in factories or hotels like slaves.

UNEQUAL SOCIETY

As India's industries have developed, it has become a wealthier country. However, this new wealth has not been shared equally between people in the cities and people in the countryside. Wealth produced by factories in the cities has been spent there, rather than in the countryside, so country people are poorer.

Cities have more schools than country areas, so city people are twice as likely to be able to read and write. Built-up areas have better health care, too. Twice as many babies die in the villages as in the cities.

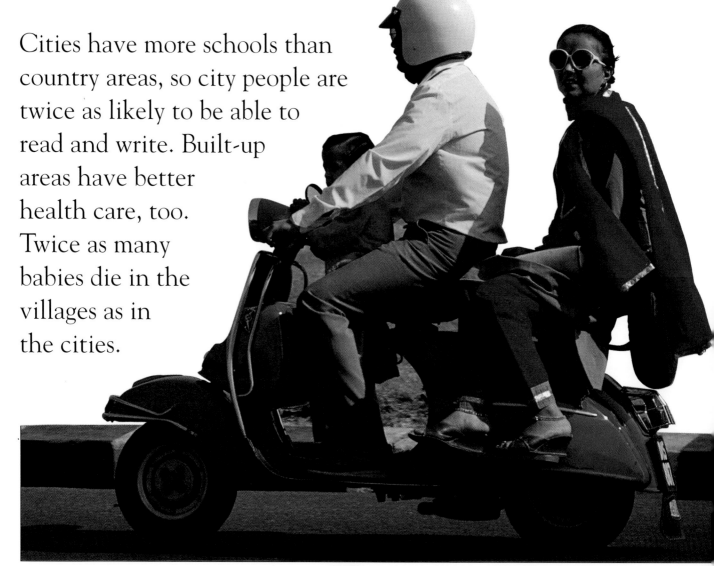

▼ Only richer city people can afford a scooter.

COUNTRY LIFE

India is a nation of country people. Nearly three-quarters of the population live in villages there.

In the villages, land is the most important possession. It provides country people with a place to graze animals and grow crops for eating or selling.

Throughout India, the land is owned unequally. A few people own a lot of land and millions have no land at all. In between these two groups are poor farmers who own tiny plots of land.

▲ A rich landowner and his family.

Many wealthy landowners use their powerful position to make more money. They rent land to landless people in return for a large share of their harvest. This leaves the farmers with barely enough food to live on.

GETTING INTO DEBT

Poor people borrow money from rich landowners. They are lent it on condition that the money is paid back at a high rate of interest. Many borrowers fall behind with their repayments and get deeper in debt. Some people's debt becomes so large that it cannot be paid off in their lifetime, so it is passed on to their children. Whole families end up working for the money lender to pay off an inherited debt.

MANY CHILDREN

Country people try to improve their lives by having many children. They think children will help them with their work, and will also look after them when they are old. But bigger families only add problems to people in the countryside.

This potter's ▶ children are helping him with his work so he can make more money.

▲ Cities have many attractions to tempt people to move there.

The more children there are in a family, the smaller the share of land each child inherits on their father's death. The less land there is, the harder it is for everyone to grow enough to eat.

MOVING TO THE CITIES

As India's cities have developed, millions of people have moved there in search of a better life. They hope for regular work in the city.

However, city life rarely lives up to the hopes of the newcomers. There are not enough factory jobs for everyone who arrives. Few country people manage to find full-time city jobs. Most end up doing part-time work or various odd jobs.

31

CITY LIFE

India's cities hold extreme wealth and extreme poverty. Millions of people are poor, but India's industries have also created a wealthy business class.

Business people have servants, smart cars, and air-conditioned homes. New shops, restaurants and hotels have opened for this new class with money to spend.

▲ These two city women live a life country people can only dream about.

THE CASTE SYSTEM

Hindus in India are divided into four social groups, or castes:

- At the top are the Brahmins, the caste from which the priests are chosen.
- Next come the Kshatriyas, the soldiers and officials.
- Then come the Vaishyas, the business and craftspeople.
- Finally, there are the Sudras, the farmers.

Separate from these castes are the Untouchables, who do the dirtiest jobs. Today, they prefer to call themselves Dalits, which means 'the oppressed'. The caste system is strongest in the countryside. In most villages, each caste has its own neighbourhood. People can only marry within their own caste.

CITY PROBLEMS

In the last 30 years, India's cities have grown very rapidly. In the ten years between 1971 and 1981 alone, they grew by 45 per cent on average. Some cities grew even faster.

CITY SLUMS

An estimated 50 million people live in slums in Indian cities.

Now the cities have reached bursting point. Power stations cannot cope with the demand for electricity. Public transport cannot deal with the number of passengers. There is a shortage of houses, so homes have become very expensive.

▼ A slum in New Delhi.

These problems affect poor people more than the wealthy business class. Millions of poor people cannot afford to buy a house, so they live on the streets, or in makeshift shacks in dirty slums.

Disabled people ▶ often beg on the streets in India, because the government has no money to look after them.

CASTE AND RELIGION

The caste system in India makes it hard for many people to improve their lives. People in the higher castes have the best chance in life. Since Independence, the government has tried to break down the inequalities caused by the caste system. But it is still harder for people from lower castes to get proper schooling and good jobs.

MAIN RELIGIONS	
Hindus	83%
Muslims	11%
Christians	2%
Sikhs	2%
Others including Buddhists	2%

Before Independence, Pakistan and Bangladesh were part of India. In 1947 they became separate nations for Muslim people. India became a mainly Hindu nation, but many Muslims still live there.

Now it is against the law to discriminate against anyone because of their religion. In practise, however, there is rivalry between the two religions, which sometimes leads to violence.

MRS INDIRA GANDHI
Indira Gandhi was the daughter of the first prime minister of independent India. She was prime minister herself from 1966–77 and from 1980–84.

▲ Indira Gandhi (bottom right) became prime minister despite the generally low status of Indian women.

WOMEN'S ROLE
Indian society has traditionally been dominated by men. In the cities, women are now more equal, but in the countryside, men still make the important decisions.

Traditionally, women do not earn money in India, so they are expected to bring wealth with them when they marry. The bride's family give the husband a dowry – presents of jewellery, furniture and clothes. Dowry payments can put many families in debt, so daughters are unpopular. Poor families do not look after girls properly, so many die.

IMPROVING PEOPLE'S LIVES

In the last 200 years, people have tried various ways to help the poor in India. Their methods have not always been successful.

Non-government organizations (NGOs) are groups who have helped India's poor since colonial times. The first NGOs opened schools, hospitals and orphanages. But they did not try to solve the social problems that caused poverty.

In the 1960s, the NGOs improved conditions in villages by digging wells and providing health care. But they still did not ask poor people themselves what they needed.

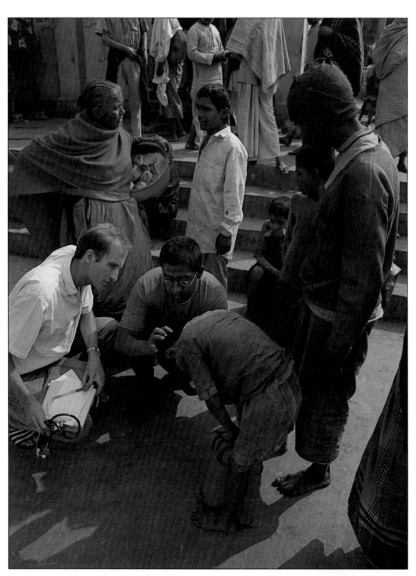

▼ A European doctor helps at a health clinic, which receives money from charities abroad.

Digging wells ▶ helps poor people, but the causes of poverty must also be tackled.

Today, people believe that the best way to tackle poverty is to ask people about their problems and let them suggest their own solutions. This means they can be helped to help themselves.

EDUCATION AND NEW SKILLS
Education helps improve people's lives. People who can read and write can read and check loan agreements, so they cannot be cheated. People who can add and subtract can check the amount of change they are given at a market.

Education helps in other ways too. Women find out about health care, so they can take better care of their families.

37

▲ These women are learning how to use sewing machines so they can start their own clothes business.

Learning a new skill such as weaving or carpentry also helps poor people improve their lives. The training will help them to get a better job, or even start their own business.

LOANS

NGOs can help poor people by providing loans at low interest rates. With an NGO loan, a newly trained tailor can buy a sewing machine without running into debt with the local money lender. A poor farmer can dig a new irrigation channel, or buy new types of seeds or fertilizers, which will help him grow better crops.

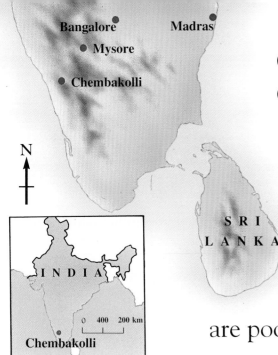

▲ Chembakolli lies in the far south of India. Mysore, the nearest big city, is 130 km away.

CHEMBAKOLLI

Chembakolli is a small village in the state of Tamil Nadu. It is home to a group of Ardivasis. The Ardivasis are a very ancient Indian people, but they are now outcasts. Over 50 million Ardivasis live in central and southern India. Most are poor, landless farmers.

Rejected by society, few Ardivasis receive good health care or a proper education. Few can read or write.

Since 1987, an Indian NGO has been helping the people of Chembakolli. It encourages the villagers to act together as a group. At village meetings called *sanghams*, people gather to list their problems, and decide on the best solutions.

◀ Villagers talk about their problems at a *sangham* in Chembakolli.

▲ Doctors visiting Chembakolli. Before help arrived, villagers had to walk many miles to get medical help.

IMPROVING LIFE IN CHEMBAKOLLI

The NGO has helped the villagers start a saving scheme. Everyone pays two rupees a month. The money is loaned out to villagers to pay off their debts and buy the things they need. The loans are repaid at a low cost.

The savings scheme is also used to pay doctors, who visit the village regularly. Trained health workers look after the people between their visits.

◄ Some villagers buy tea seedlings with a loan.

The loan scheme helps some farmers to buy tea seedlings. Tea is a good crop to sell to earn extra money.

A NEW SCHOOL
The NGO in Chembakolli has also helped to open a school. Before, a few Adivasi children went to the local government school. But they did not enjoy it because the other children made them feel inferior.

The new school is run by villagers who have now trained as teachers. They believe that school is not just about reading, writing and arithmetic. They also help Adivasi children to become more confident and take pride in their culture.

▼ Two Adivasi children at the new school.

STREET CHILDREN

All over India, street children miss out on schooling. Living on the streets with little food harms their health.

A BRIGHTER FUTURE FOR STREET CHILDREN

In Bangalore, several NGOs are working to improve the lives of street children. They have opened shelters where some of the children now live all the time. Others just visit during the day.

In the shelters, children learn skills that will help them get jobs. Some teach crafts such as carpentry and sewing, as well as feeding the children and giving health advice.

Bijl, on the left, has a ▶ better life since he started going to the shelter.

'On the streets my biggest problem was food. Now I'm in a shelter. I wear decent clothes and can eat and wash every day.'
– Bijl, aged 10.

▲ Rock-climbing and other outdoor sports help to build street children's confidence.

Teenagers over 16 go to another NGO when they have learned a skill. The staff there help them to find jobs with local firms.

The shelters help the teenagers build their confidence and learn the skills they will need to get a full-time job.

'I've been working as a garage mechanic for a year now. It's a great job and I would like to open my own garage one day. Without help, I'd still be a rag picker, and I never want to go back to that.' – **Lokech, who used to be a street child.**

THE FUTURE

▲ Tourists who visit India bring much-needed money.

▲ Ladakh, in northern India, is still a very poor region.

In 1947, few villages in India had electricity. There was very little industry, and only a small percentage of people could read and write. Since then, India has made improvements in all these areas, but poverty is still a big problem.

▲ It will take time for wealth from India's industries to reach poor people like these.

The Indian government are spending a lot of money on the country's industries. They hope that wealth created by industries will reach the poor.

FOREIGN DEBT

To develop its industries, India borrowed money from abroad. Now it owes a debt of billions of dollars. Today many people think the debts of poor countries such as India should be cancelled.

This plan will take some time to work. Until then, India's poor need help to improve their own lives.

GLOSSARY

Astronomy The study of the Sun, Moon, stars and planets.

Basic needs Things people need to survive, such as health, houses and schooling.

Caste A social group in India. Children belong to the same caste as their parents.

Colony A country that is controlled by another country.

Fertilizer Something added to the soil to make it better for growing crops.

Gross National Product (GNP) The total money a country earns inside its borders, plus the money it makes from exports.

Independent Free from foreign rule.

Inherited Received from a relative.

Interest Money that has to be paid back to pay for a loan.

Investment Putting money into a business or product so that it will flourish and make more money.

Irrigated Land that has had water added to it in order to grow crops.

Loan Money that has been borrowed.

Monsoon The name of a wind that brings heavy rain to India in summer.

Non-government organization (NGO) A group of people who do work such as helping the poor.

Plateau A flat, raised area of land.

Raw materials Materials in their natural state, such as coal or iron ore.

Recycler Someone who turns rubbish and waste into a material that can be re-used.

Repayments Sums of money used to pay back a loan.

Rickshaw A small, three-wheeled vehicle.

Saris Traditional Indian women's dress, wrapped around the body and draped over one shoulder.

Slums Poor, overcrowded housing.

Wootz High-quality Indian steel.

TOPIC WEB

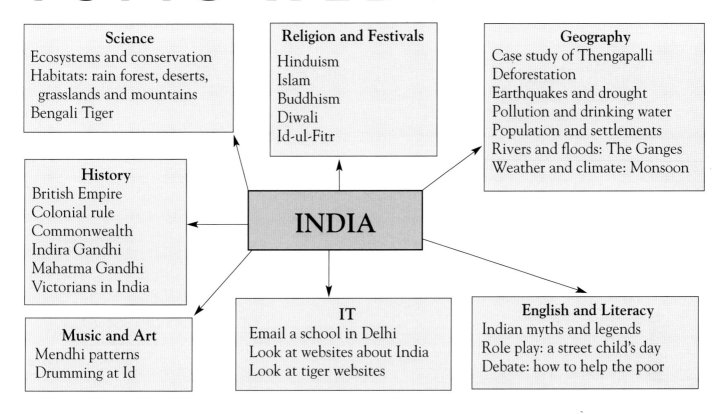

Science
Ecosystems and conservation
Habitats: rain forest, deserts, grasslands and mountains
Bengali Tiger

Religion and Festivals
Hinduism
Islam
Buddhism
Diwali
Id-ul-Fitr

Geography
Case study of Thengapalli
Deforestation
Earthquakes and drought
Pollution and drinking water
Population and settlements
Rivers and floods: The Ganges
Weather and climate: Monsoon

History
British Empire
Colonial rule
Commonwealth
Indira Gandhi
Mahatma Gandhi
Victorians in India

INDIA

Music and Art
Mendhi patterns
Drumming at Id

IT
Email a school in Delhi
Look at websites about India
Look at tiger websites

English and Literacy
Indian myths and legends
Role play: a street child's day
Debate: how to help the poor

FINDING OUT MORE

BOOKS AND PHOTOPACKS

Asia (*Continents* series) by David Lambert (Wayland, 1997)

A Flavour of India by Mike Hirst (Wayland, 1999)

Chembakolli Photopack and slide set looking at life in a village in southern India. (ActionAid)

India (*Country Fact Files* series) by Anita Ganeri (MacDonald Young Books, 1997)

India (*Country Insights* series) by David Cumming (Wayland, 1997)

India (*Cultural Journeys* series) by Paul Dash (Wayland, 1998)

Life Stories: Ghandi by Peggy Burns (Wayland, 1993)

Stories from India by Vayu Naidu (Wayland, 2000)

ADDRESSES AND WEBSITES

ActionAid, Hamlyn House, Archway, London N19 5PG. Tel 0207 282 4101
Website: www.actionaid.org

Oxfam: 274 Banbury Road, Oxford OX2 7DZ.
Tel: 01865 56777
Website: www.oxfam.org.uk

Christian Aid: PO Box 100, London SE1 7RT.
Tel: 0207 60 4444.

Development Education Association, 3rd Floor, Cowper Street, London EC2A 4AP

Save the Children Fund: Mary Datchelor House, 17 Grove Lane, London SE5 8RD. Tel: 0207 703 5400.

Unicef: 55-6 Lincoln's Inn Fields, London WC2A 3NB. Tel: 0207 405 5592
Email: info@unicef.org.uk

INDEX

Page numbers in **bold** show pictures as well as text.